The Day Trading for Beginners Guide: How to make a living on Day Trading incl. Trading Tools, Stock Market Strategies, Investment Management and Trading Psychology

William K. Bradford

ISBN- 9798670244046

Table of Contents

Chapter 1 – Introduction

If you're reading this, then welcome. You've picked up this book with an aim. A mission. A desire to take control of your life. To seek financial security. To take your career to the next level in terms of independence and success. For that, I have to salute you. You're taking a bold step that many people dream about in their lives, but not many people take the first step necessary to make it come true.

You have, and for that, you should be excited.

What you read on the following pages aims to sow the seed that will blossom into a fruitful and profitable career in the day trading industry. If you're new to the stock market, have little idea what it's about and how you can make money on it, or you've done a bit of research, and you're unsure on where to begin, then you've chosen the best book to help you on your way.

There's no denying the stock market can be a daunting and overwhelming place, especially if you're venturing in for the first time. You've probably heard stock market terms thrown about here and then, maybe through movies like the Wolf of Wall Street, or in the media after the 2008 stock market crash. It's interesting because whichever way you look at the mainstream image of the stock market, you always see it as an extreme.

There's the Wall Street of the 80s where everyone was hyped on narcotics, shouting at each other in crazy ways but making millions, or you hear about stockbrokers investing millions and losing everything in an overnight blip of which the damage ripples out to markets around the world. You rarely hear about what's happening in the middle.

Of course, we're talking about the thousands of investors who aren't the extreme examples. The investors who invest in stocks part-time or full-time. The investors who have built their portfolios up from scratch over the last few years and decades, now comfortably living on the money they're making from their investments.

These are people making tens of thousands, or even hundreds of thousands, a year. With hard work, discipline, patience, and grafting, they now reap the many benefits that come with this kind of career. Financial security. The ability to put money aside for themselves, their children, their family, and their retirement. The people who can comfortably buy a new car, move up the property ladder, and go on a vacation without it being too much of a financial strain.

This is precisely where we aim to get you within the following pages of this book.

Within the following chapters, we're going to be exploring a select type of stock market investment known as 'Day Trading'. You can do this part-time or full-time, or part-time going into a full-time career, and if you're any good, you can end up making a very substantial amount of money.

Now, don't get your hopes up in the sense that we're going to teach you how to make millions. While that's entirely possible, this will take years of investments and a lot of experience on your behalf. What we're aiming to do is to get you off to the best possible start we can, helping you go from someone with no experience to an investor that knows exactly what they need to be doing.

Are you ready to start your own day trading investment journey? Let's get into it.

Chapter 2 – Day Trading as a Full-Time Career

First things first, let's get on the same page. Day Trading, as the name suggests, is the investment process of sitting at a computer throughout the day and trading securities on the stock market. Back in the well-known days of Wall Street, trading used to take place on a floor of a brokerage, trading house, or the larger financial institutions. Here, people would manually buy and sell stocks in what can only be described as chaos.

However, since technology has come so far over the last thirty years, it's now much easier for anyone to get access to the stock market to make purchases and investments using only their computer. In fact, if you really wanted too, you could become a full-time day trader using only your smartphone, but let's not get ahead of ourselves.

The stock market is only open during set hours of the day, so a day trader is someone who operates within these hours. They are different to most investors because a typical investor may spend $10,000 in stock and then will hold onto it for five years while waiting for it to make a profit. A day trader, on the other hand, can buy and sell multiple stocks over the course of a day.

The value of stock and other securities on the stock market is changing all the time, and you only have to do a quick online search for any stock, and you can see the variety of value stock can have over 24 hours. However, there are endless strategies you can use to make money, but we'll go into all that as the book progresses.

Some believe that day trading can be a little controversial, and this is something you'll need to be aware of. For this reason, it's actually one of the most debated subjects in Wall Street, although it's easy to get confused about what is going on.

Since the rise of the internet, there are plenty of scams and people out there who are trying to mislead investors with the aim of basically stealing their investment money. If you're researching strategies and you see an investment that's too good to be true, the chances are it probably is. When it comes to making money on the stock market, there's no get rich quick schemes out there.

Making money through stocks, whether you're a long-term investor or a day trader, is all about making lots of little successful decisions that will build up and stack over time, ultimately creating a lot of financial wealth for yourself.

So, is it possible to day trade as your full-time career? Yes, it is, but don't believe it's going to be a smooth ride. You need to make sure you're investing time in educating yourself and getting to know the market and what tools are available to you. In many ways, especially educationally and emotionally, day trading can sometimes be far more demanding than a traditional day job.

If you're choosing whether day trading is for you, here are some things to think about.

The Advantages of Day Trading

All the benefits you'd expect to come with becoming a full-time day trader are very much real. By going full time, you end up becoming your own boss, and you can set your own working hours. This is ideal if you want to spend time with your family and want the freedom to do what you want whenever you want.

It's also so much more affordable than starting most other kinds of business in terms of overheads. You don't need to rent or buy an expensive commercial property, nor do you need to invest in stocks, equipment, machinery, or staff. Think how much you currently spend on fuel or transport costs for commuting to work, and how much time in your life you spend convoying back and forth.

As a day trader, all you need is a computer with an internet connection, and you're ready to go. This means you can work at home, in your local café, or anywhere you want in the world. You can work in complete comfort as and when you want, in a way that suits you.

What's more, there is basically an infinite number of ways you can pay the stock market game, so whether you're looking to turn trading into a bit of a side-hustle, or you're looking to make millions and really go for gold, there's the opportunity to do it all in a way that works for you.

The Disadvantages of Day Trading

While all the benefits of day trading are very lucrative, it's important to remember that it's not all sunshine and rainbows. Day trading tends to be a somewhat lonesome activity in the sense that you can spend hours sitting at home on your own, staring at a computer screen. There's no colleagues or office chat, but you can overcome this if you're with your family or join day trader social groups online.

Of course, the main disadvantage is that you're not making a set salary and your finances can be up and down, especially when you're starting. One day you could make $5,000 and the next you're losing $3,000. It's inconsistent. Once you start making money and putting some aside (we'll talk more about this when getting set up in the following chapters), you'll be fine, but when you're getting going there's a genuine risk you could be losing money.

Bear all these points in mind when it comes to choosing whether the path of day trader is for you. There's definitely excitement and thrills to be had when becoming a day trader, and it can be extremely profitable when done right. You just need to make sure you keep your calm and do everything you can to make the right decisions.

And don't worry; we're going to show you how to do this right now.

Chapter 3 – How Do You Make Money Day Trading?

One of the most important decisions you'll need to make when you're starting your journey is what kind of securities you're going to be trading. For this, you'll need to think about what kind of markets interest you. Do you have any passions or interests that have made you want to get involved in the stock market already? Do you have any preferences as to what you're trading?

Some examples of what you can trade are as follows;

- Stocks

- Cryptocurrencies

- Forex

- CFDs

- Gold and other precious metals

- Commodities

When choosing what you want to be trading, you need to be thinking about what kind of risk you're accepting into your career. Some markets are more volatile than others and will experience much more drastic change, which of course can be both good and bad, depending on what investments you've made.

For example, the cryptocurrency market is massively volatile. The Bitcoin market can rise and fall dramatically over the course of a day, a month, and a year, meaning many people have made tremendous gains and profits, whereas others have faced jaw-dropping losses. It's the same for company stocks. Some stocks are incredibly risky the same as there are stocks that are considered low risk.

There are clear examples of this. If you're trading in tech stocks, the price of these securities can rise and fall dramatically. You can never really be sure whether it's going to go up or down, and an investment here may leave you short of money over the long-term. However, with significant risks come the opportunities for significant gains.

On the other hand, if you're trading in a commodity stock like a retail outlet or food, an essential stock that commonly remains the same in the market because it's a commodity everyone consistently. These are considered low-risk stocks and tend to be better suited for stable long-term growth investments strategies.

What you decide to trade in is really up to you. Still, for the purpose of simplicity, we're going to be focusing on buying and selling traditional stocks for the remainder of this ebook, but feel free to apply the same tactics and strategies to any other kind of security you're looking to trade.

How to Make Money Day Trading Stocks

Before we go any further and start your journey as a day trader, we just want to explore how money is actually made. A straightforward example of this would be that you wake up when the markets open and find a stock you like the look of (how you choose stocks we'll look at later).

You buy the stock at $5 per piece and watch it throughout the day. As the day goes on, the stock price rises until around 2 pm when the stock has gone up to $5.50, so you sell them. Since you invested $5,000 in stock at the beginning of the trading day, you've just made $500 on that investment.

Since you'll have multiple investments on the go at any one time and they will rise and fall at variable rates, this is how you can make a lot of money over the course of a day. With this in mind, this is where your journey into the world of becoming a day trader really begins.

Chapter 4 - Getting Ready for Your Day Trading Career

Welcome to the beginning of the rest of your life. This is the chapter where we talk about how to get your life ready for becoming a day trader, organising everything you need to get yourself off to the best possible start. This will be a rather lengthy chapter because there's a lot to cover, including making sure you're cut out to be a trader, setting up your trading space, getting your finances in order, and getting ready to go. Here we go.

Is Day Trading Right for You?

This is an important question you need to ask yourself.

Using the questions detailed above; you need to make sure you're going to be committed to becoming a day trader. You must understand you're going to be working long hours, and you don't precisely get holiday breaks since you're your own boss and you're working for yourself.

You will also need to make sure you're not an emotionally reactive kind of person. It's absolutely guaranteed that at some point during your career, you're going to invest in a stock and you're going to lose money on it. That's just the way the game works, and it's inevitable.

However, if you're an emotional person and you lose a significant investment sum that causes you to freak out, you can bet you're going to make some bad decisions in the future. Likewise, there are going to be times when you win big money, and it's easy to get excited and want to invest more and make more. This is called greed and can backfire just as badly.

Being a day trader means being able to stand calm and relaxed in even the most stressful of situations, removing emotion from your decision-making process, sticking to your plan, and remaining grounded. If you're not this sort of person, or you can't cultivate this kind of mindset, then day trading is probably not for you.

Setting Up Your Finances

Being able to manage your finances is vital before you set into the world of day trading. If you have any kind of debt right now, you shouldn't even consider day trading until you've cleared it. If you have a loan or credit card, or both, where you're paying back interest rates of 20%, and you're only making 5% return on your investments, then you're going to be losing money.

Instead, make sure you're paying off all your debts and then getting your capital ready. This way, you'll be minimising how much interest you're paying on your credit and debt, and then maximising your profits when you start investing.

Once you're in the green, you need to start thinking about getting your capital in place. This is the starting amount of money you're going to be investing with. This can vary dramatically depending on your personal situation, so it's really up to you. You could start small, perhaps with $5,000 and then day trade part-time. As your capital grows over time, you can then begin transitioning over to becoming a full-time trader.

On the other hand, you may want to save up a lump sum that means you can quit your job and start investing straight away, although that's not recommended since you'll have no experience. Even if you have a lump sum, start small, so you can teach yourself the ropes of trading, and then start investing more and more once you start gathering experience.

Van Tharp, one of the top day traders in the world and author of Trade Your Way to Financial Freedom, recommends that if you're trading full-time, you're going to want around $100,000 to start with. If you're looking to day trade effectively, you're going to want approximately $10,000 in your trading account at all times.

The final financial aspect you'll want to consider is getting yourself a rainy-day emergency fund. This means creating a savings account where you put a recommended three months' worth of living expenses into an account and then leave it.

This means when you're trading, and if you ever come across a time in your life where you're suffering from financial difficulties, you'll have this fund to fall back on. However, you need to remember this is not an account you can ever use for trading or investment. If you have a hard-losing streak and you need money to live on to support yourself and your family, you don't want to end up with nothing. This is a financial crisis you'll want to avoid at all costs, which is why it's best to be as prepared as possible.

Learn About Stock Market Trading

This should go without saying, but if you want to become a day trader, you need to have some kind of passion or interest in the stock market world, or at least the drive to become educated about it. You need to learn when the stock market trading hours are and how the processes and systems within the stock market work.

You should have an interest in a particular niche or industry you want to trade in, and you better have some kind of passion surrounding it because you're going to need to be watching the news on this industry, reading articles and books on the subjects, and investing your time watching interviews and learning about these stock market companies in terms of how they work and what they're up too on a daily basis.

You'll also need to learn about what stocks actually, as well as other potential trading options, such as ETFs, options, futures, and mutual funds. We'll briefly describe each one in the table below, but it's crucial you take time developing a clear understanding of each other before you start implementing a trading strategy and investing in one.

Stocks	When the ownership of a company or organisation is broken down into all the shares, these are individually known as "stocks". Each stock represents a fractional ownership of a company, relative to the number of shares it has in total.
ETFs	The term shortened for 'Exchanged-Traded Funds', ETFs are a type of investment fund that is traded identically to a stock on the stock market and exchanges of the world. ETFs are indexes made of other securities and assets, such as stocks, special funds, and commodity funds.
Options	Options is the term given to a contract that gives a specific buyer a right to buy or sell any underlying asset, although it doesn't guarantee an obligation for a sale. However, options will give the price that must be valid prior to or on a specified date stated on the option contract.

Futures	Futures are another type of contract that point to the legal agreement that contracts the buying and selling of something at a price, time, and date that has been predetermined. However, these metrics won't be known by the parties involved and is classed as an asset.
Mutual Funds	Mutual funds are investment portfolios that are managed by professional financial services. These services bring in money from several investors to buy stocks, shares, and other securities, like the ones in this table.
Gold & Precious Metals	Gold (and sometimes other precious metals) refers to the trading asset of the metal gold that is stored in banks around the US, and around the world.
Eminis	Eminis are another type of futures contracts that track the S&P 500 stock index market. It is also known as the E-Mini, ES, or just Mini.

Cryptocurrencies	This is a broad term that refers to the trade of cryptocurrencies within the stock market. This can be done individually or via an exchange.
Forex	Forex is the trading of foreign currencies around the world by converting one currency into another and then continuing to trade in this manner.

Practice Your Money Management Skills

The last thing you need to do before you even start to think about getting ready to trade stocks is to consider how effective your money management skills are. If you're thinking to yourself 'yeah, my money management skills are pretty good', then take a step back and consider how you can improve. There's always room to be better, and as a day trader, these are improvements you're going to both want and need.

Consider this. If you're starting with $100,000 and you're using a tried-and-tested strategy that has a 60% success rate, how much are you going to invest to begin with? What happens if your first four trades fail and come out as a loss? How should you be allocating your capital?

With any kind of trading, it's always a good idea to start small and then expand over time. It's rather stupid to jump in on your first trade and buy $100,000 worth of stock and just hope for the best. Of course, it might pay off, but if you're being this risky with your first investment, the chances are it's going to backfire dramatically later down the line.

Work on your money management skills and nurture the ability to step back and make decisions from a grounded state of mind. You need to be able to wisely select which opportunities you're going to invest in and how you're going to manage your investment capital. Even if you're using a strategy that has a 30% success rate, you can still make a large amount of profit from it when you have proper money management skills.

Once you've developed all these aspects of your life and you've got yourself ready, you're one step closer to starting your day trading career. Before we really jump into the meat of what you need to do and actually start investing, there's one more aspect we need to cover, and that's developing your day trading mindset.

Chapter 5 - Developing a Day Trading Mindset

The truth is that anyone can be a day trader. You're not born with inherent abilities that make you a better or worse day trader than the next person. The difference between a lousy day trader and a successful one is that the successful one has put the time and energy into developing their mindset into one that works.

Day traders aren't born. They're specially trained.

If you're looking to be a successful day trader, and why wouldn't you be, then you need to be working hard of developing a successful mindset. There are several traits which can be a part of this kind of mindset, so we're going to focus on the most important ones you need to be thinking about and implementing into your own life.

Discipline

Let's start with the most important. Discipline. Of course, discipline is vital, and if you've been following along with this book in order, then you'll know why. The stock market offers a basically infinite playing field in which to trade any way you want, and you can make changes to your strategy at any second of any day.

However, this means there's an infinite number of chances to screw up and make a mistake, which is why being disciplined is key. Let's say you stumble across a fantastic stock opportunity and you think it could make you a serious amount of money. What do you do?

Do you;

A. Take all your investments out of other stocks, sell everything, and fully invest in this new opportunity?

B. Forget about the opportunity. It's still a risk.

C. Stick to your investment strategy and invest the same amount as you would as any other stock. If it's an excellent opportunity, then you're still going to profit.

Of course, the disciplined answer is C. If you see an excellent opportunity and you're not disciplined, you could end up investing everything you have. If it doesn't pay off, then you've just severely damaged yourself and your capital for nothing.

Being a successful day trader is all about being disciplined enough to stick with your plan, to stick with your investment strategy, and not make silly mistakes because you're getting away in the excitement of a good opportunity. The same applies if you're having a losing streak.

You need discipline there to make sure you're not jumping your guns and making panic-based decisions that could do more harm than good. Always have the self-control to stick with your strategy.

Patience

Hand in hand with the discipline mindset above, you need to make sure you're exercising patience. It's very tempting to make quick decisions based on the unfolding trends of the market, which can rapidly change on a minute by minute basis, but you can't.

What you need to be successful is the ability to remain patient until the right time has come to buy or sell, and then having the discipline to carry out the transaction without second-guessing yourself or coming up with other decisions that aren't a part of your strategy.

Flexible and Adaptable

A key component of being a successful day trader. The markets are changing all the time, and they're not always going to be working in your favour nor aligned with your strategy. Sometimes an industry is going to be healthy and confident, and sometimes it's going to be weak and volatile.

To a successful trader, this doesn't matter because they'll be adaptable enough to stick with their strategy and make it work in any condition. No matter when happens when you log onto your account into the morning, you need to be able to see what's going on and make decisions accordingly, all in real-time, all with the discipline and patience we spoke about above.

The Ability to Detach from Emotions

We've mentioned this already, but when it comes to becoming a day trader, you need the ability to leave your emotions at the door and have a degree of mental toughness against whatever happens. When you're winning big, you need to remain natural, and the same applies when you're losing hard.

Think of it this way, the most successful traders, when compared to unsuccessful traders, will win slightly more on their wins, and lose marginally less on their losses. That's it. That's all there is to being a successful trader. It's not about doubling down on one stock and trying to get a 100% return on your investment.

It's about making 1%-10% here and there on both your wins and losses. If you're getting carried away in the moment, you're going to end up making rash decisions which could cost you so much in the long-term, and it's not worth harming your portfolio in this way.

As before, you're going to experience losing streaks. It's going to happen. During these times, you need to be proactive in minimising your losses as much as possible by staying focused and on task. As soon as you lose your mind and lose your cool, it's game over, and you could throw away your entire career in a few careless trades.

Being Able to Think Forward

As a day trader, you're not going to be successful if you can't get your head out of the past. Yes, not every trade you make is going to pay off and you're going to make mistakes. That can't be avoided. However, if you're mulling on past mistakes and you can't seem to move on, this is going to hold you back from your full potential.

The only reason you ever need to look back to the past is to take your experiences and learn from them. You need to be thinking about the future, what you want to achieve, and what decisions you can make to get there. You're always planning your next move and calculating what you can do to make the most of the market's opportunities.

With this in mind, it goes without saying that day traders need to be forward thinkers. You'll be prepared for any eventuality, and you'll have a plan on what you're going to do whether the market goes up or down. This kind of mindset is critical if you want to make it in the world of stock market investment.

Taking Responsibility

Of course, you're going to get help with your trading. You'll read books, like this one, talk with other traders, watch videos and read articles, and maybe even get a mentor to help you along the way. However, when you put all that to the side, it is you and you alone who will be clicking the buttons and making the trades.

Whether things go right or wrong, it is you that is responsible for making those decisions, and it's vital for you to accept that this is how it works, and this level of independence is your own. Sure, there's nothing wrong with learning as much as you can from other people, but there comes a time where you'll need to go it alone and make decisions for yourself.

Put it this way, let's say you've been following someone for some time and copying what they're doing, but they give up day trading, or the service you're using shuts down, and you now need to go it alone. You'll regret never taking the time to learn for yourself, and you'll be learning the lesson of independence the hard way.

The best thing to do is to start being as independent as possible from early on and then building it up slowly. That doesn't mean you can't learn from people, but don't just copy and emulate people. Learn from them and take these lessons and apply them to your own investment and trading practices.

These are the very core mindset traits you'll need to be paying attention to and developing in order to become a successful day trader. Nurturing these mindset traits and abilities won't happen overnight. It will come with experience, so make sure you're being open and mindful that this is the case, rather than storming into the world of investment with your eyes and ears closed.

Chapter 6 - How to Create Your Day Trading Set Up

Okay, so your life is in check and ready to go, you've sorted out your finances, and you've collected your capital and your starting investment, and your mindset is in check and ready to rumble. Now is when you can start truly thinking about making your first investments.

In this chapter, we're going to explore how you can set up your equipment at home to start day trading, what accounts you need to trade stocks and shares, and how you can start making money. By the end of this chapter, you'll be absolutely ready to purchase any stock you want and can start making money.

Setting Up Your Desk

The first thing you need to do is get your desk set up. If you're working from home, I recommend setting up a dedicated area in your house to work. You're more than welcome to work on your laptop from your bed or sit at your kitchen table, but this makes it very difficult to cultivate a proper work-life balance.

Having a dedicated space means as soon as you go into this space, your mind goes into work mode, and you can solely focus on what you're doing. The same applies when you leave. While your day of trading could be incredibly stressful, being able to leave the room and switch off is key to maintaining a healthy mindset.

If you're working at home and you have a family, you'll also want to work away from them because you can't have them distracting you. This is why it's also a good idea to potentially leave your phone in another room, and minimise distractions, such as having televisions or games consoles.

Next, you'll want to set up your computer. Since you'll be working online, it really doesn't matter what equipment you have, but anything too old could be a bit too slow and unreliable. You want a mid-range laptop that's capable of displaying all your facts and figures and has a minimum of a 4GB hard drive and at least a four-core processor.

It's also highly recommended you get an HDMI cable-enabled device.

This is because you're then going to want to get yourself a television screen or second monitor. By connecting your computer and extending your desktop to the second monitor, you'll be able to display financial news channels, real-time stock exchange websites, and news reports, all without having to keep clicking back and forth between multiple tabs.

The recommended minimum screen size you get is around 24-inches, and anything bigger is a bonus. The bigger the screen, the more you'll be able to see and the more information you'll be able to monitor in real-time. The last essential you'll want to think about is a steady and reliable internet connection.

Go for the best internet connection you can afford. This means you want fast upload and download speeds and the maximum uptime. If you can, use an ethernet cable instead of using wireless connections. You don't want to be halfway through a trade when your internet cuts out.

Also, make sure you out the internet router in your office. You don't want anybody outside the room having internet troubles just to reset the router during a critical transaction, upload, or deposit.

This is the bare minimum setup you'll want to be thinking about getting.

Choosing a Broker That Works for You

Next, once your office is all set up, you'll want to be thinking about what day trading broker you're going to be working with. There are plenty of brokers out there for you to choose from and which one you end up with will depend on your personal requirements.

In a nutshell, these are the conditions you want to be looking out for.

- The fees of the broker

- The minimum account deposit feature

- What you're able to trade

- How hard or easy the service is to use

- How much data you can stream

- How much you can customise your experience

- The terms and conditions for using the broker

- What payment options are available

- How secure the broker service is

If you want to get started for the first time, which if you're reading this then you are, and you don't have much budget to invest, you'll want a broker that offers a $0 minimum account deposit. You'll also want to check out what fees your chosen broker provides. Some will offer $0 on fees whereas some will charge.

However, what makes most brokers different from one another is the features that they offer. Some will allow you to trade stocks and shares, but won't provide trading services from futures, options, or cryptocurrencies.

More premium brokers will allow you to stream multiple lines of data into your account, so you can see what's going on, whereas more affordable and easier to use accounts will only offer a single stream.

Since you're just starting out, we highly recommend you go for a beginner-friendly broker with minimal fees and deposit limits. This way, you can start to gain experience with using a broker account and can really start to get the hang of what they have to offer.

There's no hard and fast rule on which broker you should use, and there's no limits on the number of accounts you can have. So, once you've mastered the basics on a beginner-friendly account, you can then begin to scale and upgrade to a more feature-rich broker, once you know what you're doing.

Brokers can change their fees and terms and conditions all the time, so make sure you're researching brokers at the time you're ready to create an account either using comparison websites. You could always head over to the individual broker websites and directly see what they have to offer.

Next, you want to see what payment options the website lets you deal with, and what kind of deposit and withdraw limits they're working with. Check if you're using debit or Visa cards, PayPal, Western Union, Sage, American Express, or any other kind of payment platform, and make sure the broker you're using is compatible with what you have.

The last feature you'll want to look for is security. Of course, you don't want to be using a dodgy broker website that doesn't offer you top of the range security. 256-bit encryption is the leading standard, and you should never settle for less. Think about how much money you're transferring and imagine using an unsecured website and all that money going missing.

Makes me shiver just thinking about it, but it does happen to people, so be careful.

Remember, if you come across any broker websites that claim they're going to be able to help you get rich quickly, then this is almost certainly a scam. You should never create an account, nor enter your financial details into these broker websites. Avoid them at all costs.

You be wondering if you can day trade on a traditional broker account, and you can, which gives you access to a full range of brokerage services, but there is one condition. You must maintain having $25,000 in your account. Otherwise, day trading services will not be available to you.

There are loopholes you can use, such as only making three trades over a five-day period, not trading on US stock marketers, or opening multiple accounts, but if you don't reach the $25,000 limit, your best bet is to open a special day trading account.

Creating Your Digital Trading Account

Once you've chosen a broker that works for you, you'll need to create an account. This is a simple step where you just click the sign-up button and work your way through the sign-up process.

Once you've signed up and confirmed your account, you'll need to make a deposit into your account, unless you're using a premium broker who will have asked you to do it already on sign up. Deposit your money, and that's it.

As soon as the money is in your broker account, you're ready to start trading stocks!

Chapter 7 - Two Vital Tools You Need for Day Trading

If you want to start trading stocks straight away, then go ahead and skip this chapter. The previous chapters will have already set you up with everything you need. However, if you're looking to take your trading to the best possible level, then make sure you stick around as we're going to explore the three essential tools you need to have in addition to your computer and internet connection.

Sure, everything you need to do can be done from your office, but having these tools will help enhance your experience, will give you access to more real-time information you need to make real-time decisions, and make real-time money.

We're going to be focusing on two of these essential tools to get you started, but as you learn to grow and develop your own style of trading, don't be afraid to branch out and create a setup that is suited to your own way of doing things.

Dedicated Day Trading Charting Software

Being able to monitor and interact with trading charts is the blood of what you'll be doing as a day trader. Being able to see what the markets are doing and seeing the information update every second is key to be able to make timely and precise trading decisions each and every day.

There are many brokers out there that will offer their own graphing systems, or you could monitor them live in your browser. Still, no graphing experience will come close to those provided by a dedicated graphing software application.

Using graphing software, you'll be able to track and analyse the price charts, as well as being able to customise your dashboard so you can stack graphs that you're interested in side-by-side, rather than having to switch through multiple tabs and potentially miss your opportunities.

Using this software means you can quickly search up and pull any graphs you want to know, and you'll have multiple options to see tick and timed charts, as well as breaking them down into 1 to 5-minute time charts, hourly charts, and more.

Of course, there's charting software out there that's designed for all kinds of traders, so you'll be looking specifically for day trader-friendly software. These are applications that allow you to make traders as quickly as possible and can be customised to suit your needs.

It can pay to research what software out there will suit your personal needs and requirements, shortlisting a couple you like and then trialling them to see which one is best for you. There's no right or wrong answer as to which is best; it all depends on what you're personally looking for.

The Most Up to Date Market Data

Being able to trade accurately and precisely means being able to stay up to date with the latest news and streams of financial data. If you're not buying with accurate data, you're going to be making purchasing decisions that aren't accurate.

Of course, your chosen broker will be providing you with financial data as and when it comes in, but you can take this one step further by gathering information yourself and in much more detail.

Specific whether you're trading in NYSE or NASDAQ stock exchanges and get yourself access to Level II data. In trading, Level I data is the basic data your broker will give you, and all the chart software will offer this kind of data for you to base your trading decisions off of.

Level I data consists of the following;

Bid Price	This refers to the highest posted and public price that someone is willing to buy a stock for.
The Size of the Bid	The number of shares, stocks, contracts, forex lots, or other securities that are publicly being bid for at the bid price.
The Asking Price	This is the lowest price in which the seller of an asset is prepared to sell. For example, a company's asking price for a share of their company.
The Asking Size	The size of the lot containing shares, forex lots, and contracts that are being sold at the asking price.
The Last Price	The last price figure that was set when the last transaction occurred.
The Last Size	The size of the lot that was last sold, containing shares, forex lots, and more.

However, Level II data takes a much more in-depth look into the markets, and if you want to precise, this is the data you'll want to be looking at. Included in this stream of data, you'll find things like;

The Highest Bid Prices	This data will show between five and 15 of the last biggest bid prices to take place on an order. This figure allows you to see all the bids that have taken place, and all the bids below it. This means you'll be able to see exactly what's going on and what figures are being moved around.
The Bid Sizes	Similar to Level I data, this should the number of shares, contracts, and forex lots, etc, that people are trying to buy at bid prices.
Lowest Asking Prices	Opposite to the highest bid prices (surprise surprise), this data shows the lowest five to 15 prices in which traders are willing to sell at for a specific asset.
The Ask Sizes	Simply the number of shares, contracts, and forex lots that are available at the asking prices.

By researching this data as a day trader, you'll be able to see exactly what's going on within a company, within several organisations, and across the business landscape, thus helping you to explore why prices of stock are changing like they are. Ultimately, this will help you react with your trading decisions in the most educated way possible.

If you're taking advantage of both these data sets, you'll be maximising your opportunities as a trader and quickly putting yourself ahead of many of the other traders out there. The more you can set yourself up for success, the possibilities you'll have to get there. Now, let's get on with some actual trading!

Chapter 8 - Choosing Your First Day Trading Stocks

Now comes the exciting part of the process; choosing the stocks you want to work with.

This is where you can get creative and start using your knowledge and experience to make decisions that are actually going to make you money. This is the crème de la crème part of being a day trader, and the choices you make now will either make you or break you. Some might even say that this is where the fun begins.

Don't worry; it's exciting, and I know you're wondering, so, which stocks do I choose?

In this chapter, we're going to be going through just that. We'll talk about the process of choosing stocks and detailing some tips to help you get going and make that all-important first purchase.

Consider Your Personal Life and Passions

Easily the best place to start is looking into your own life and seeing what you're interested in! What areas of the world are you excited about, or what industries really catch your eye? Are you a lover of tech and you're always researching about the very latest technology that's coming out? Do you love keeping your eye on and tracking the energy sector of the world? Do you follow any particular companies, or have personal values you'd like to reflect in the stocks you buy?

Answering these questions is always the best place to start because if you're choosing to work with stocks that you simply don't care about, you're not going to have a good time on the market and you're not going to stick at being a day trader for very long. Always pick stocks you have a passion for. After all, you're going to spend a lot of time learning and educating yourself of these industries, so it will pay to have an interest.

That being said, you'll want to make sure you're not emotionally attached or invested in the stocks you're choosing. Remember, at the end of the day, you're here to look at graphs and patterns to make a profit.

Choose High Liquidity Stocks

Liquidity is the term given to the process of how quickly an asset can be sold and bought on the market, and this, of course, affects the price of a stock on a day-to-day market. This is vital for day trading because if a stock takes too long to process or there's complications with the transactions, you could miss trading windows and you'll be out of a profit opportunity.

There are other benefits you can enjoy when trading liquid stocks, such as the fact they're typically discounted so you can get to save money when purchasing them. They tend to mostly be offered by companies with high market caps, which means you'll be getting more for your money.

Check Out the Trading Volume Index

The Trading Volume Index otherwise referred to as the TVI, is one of the most common indexes used by day traders to see whether you want to buy a stock or not. How this index works is by tracking how much money is moving both in and out of any particular asset.

So, in terms of stock, this refers to how much volume of a particular stock you're looking at is traded and sold within any given time period, in this case, a day. If you're seeing a specific stock is being purchased far more than usual, then you know that there's a lot of activity surrounding this stock and it's probably one you're going to want to look at for yourself.

Likewise, if a lot of buyers are selling a stock you have, this could be a clear sign that the price is about to drop, and you may want to consider selling. Remember, it's up to you to make your own decision, so you shouldn't just follow the market and what they are doing. There's plenty of traders out there that will panic buy and sell, so instead use this index as a guideline to help you stay up to date with what's going on.

Invest in Social Media Stocks

Day traders have always been drawn to social media stocks due to their high trading volumes. While some social media stocks can be somewhat volatile, there's no denying there's money to be made here, and it's one you'll want to think about investing in yourself, especially if you have an interest in social media tech companies and the marketplace.

Invest in Financial Services

Hand in hand with social media stocks, another popular stock for day traders comes in the form of financial services. In fact, many day traders will consider these stocks as some of the best. Think the Bank of America and these kinds of stocks. The stock volumes are high, and while they can be volatile, all stocks can be, it's just about making the right choices at the right time.

Some other financial services you may want to consider include;

- Morgan Stanley

- Wells Fargo

- JP Morgan

- Chase

- Citigroup

These are just some of the ways you can pick stocks, and the truth is, there are practically infinite ways to go about it. It all depends on your strategies and the approach you want to take, which brings us nicely onto our next chapter that you need to know about.

Chapter 9 - Tips on How to Choose the Best Stocks for You

Before we move on to developing your stock strategies, we're just going to take a moment, well, a chapter, to think about how you can go about choosing the right stocks. It's all well and good reading a news report that says 'yes, this stock is going to go up today', but what's the difference between a good stock and a bad stock, and how do you know whether it's right for you.

Whereas in the last chapter we looked at day trading specifics, this chapter will more about general tricks and tips you should think about when selecting your specific stocks to work with. Let's find out.

The Standard Way of Looking for Stocks

By far the most accessible way you'll start choosing stocks is just by looking at the graphs in front of you. If you see a stock which is on the up and you see it rising, you could put money into that stock, watch it grow a bit more, and then sell it. This is just a little way of making money. After all, even if you're making 1% on your deal, that's 1% more profit than you had to begin with.

We mention this practice because you'll be incorporating it into the other practices we'll talk about below. It's just important to remember you're not just looking into stocks that you have a good feeling for. The most successful stock traders will be informed and educated with their decision, but just keep an eye open for new opportunities is also part of the game.

Follow the Story of a Stock

This is the leading way you're going to be wanting to choose a stock. Every day, you need to get up, get to work, and start getting up to date with what is going on within your niche or industry. For example, let's say you're buying stocks in the tech industry.

You need to be on social media following companies on the stock exchange you're interested in, looking at stock websites, watching news programs, reading articles, and watching interviews. The more information you have, the more educated your purchasing decision will.

In this example, you've been following Samsung, and you know they're bringing out a new phone next week. You buy stocks perhaps earlier that week or the week before, you wait until release day, and there you have it. Profit. However, this is a straightforward way the story could play out.

Let's say you've been following the news and Samsung is not looking forward to releasing. They're behind on production, and they've had problems with logistics and acquiring the computer chips they need for their devices. This is sending the stock plummeting. What do you do?

Do you not buy the stock because Samsung is having problems and you think the product launch is going to flop? Do you buy the stocks when the news of all the issues come out because you believe the value is going to soar again? Do you wait and see if the stock starts to rise again and then buy to ride the wave as the stock hopefully peaks as the value returns to normal?

Of course, these are the decisions that are up to you and will be the decisions where you make or break with your profits. There are lots of considerations, such as public opinion on the company, the expert opinions, and the reputation of the company, the industry, and the stock itself, but we'll talk about these momentarily.

The point is, if you weren't researching and keeping up to date with the latest trends then you're going to be missing out on what's happening, and you won't be able to make informed purchasing decisions.

Choosing Trustworthy Information Sources

As you can see from the point above, getting information is the key to maximising your chances of success. However, this will only work if you're getting your information from trustworthy and reliable places. Where there's money in the world, there's scams, and there's unfortunately a ton of websites out there that don't care about your investment, they just want your money from you directly, or through ads.

These websites are prone to putting up fake news on the stock market, trying to manipulate the markets through false information, or just want to speculate to drive traffic so they can receive money from their ad programs. If you're basing your purchases off information from these sources, then you're going to have a bad time.

There are a few ways to check to ensure you're getting information from a trustworthy place.

Firstly, does it look legitimate? What does your common sense say about the source? Does the website or source you're looking at look authentic, or does it look like someone has just thrown the website together for no good reason? Hand in hand with this, is the source an authority source within the financial industry, like a big journalist company or media outlet?

When looking through the content, do the claims come with links you can follow? If a piece is reporting something important, then it must have links. Otherwise, it's not to be trusted. Sometimes, it may look like a website has links, but if you click through and it just takes you to another article on the same website or by the same writer. If you find this to be the case, you're better off avoiding the website at all costs and taking your research elsewhere.

You can also lookup the writer or the content creator who's written the post. If the person is unheard of or has a bad reputation, then you know you'll probably need to avoid them entirely too. At the end of the day, make sure you're being cautious and aware of what sources of information you're using and how credible they are before making a purchase.

Find Specific Companies

One of the best ways to find stocks to buy and sell within the industry you're working with is to simply list up a load of companies you want to trade between, and then only trade between these companies. After all, if you want to learn all about individual companies and make educated decisions, then you're probably only going to want to get a list of dedicated companies because you can't learn everything about them all!

The first place you can start is looking into an ETF, which stands for exchange-traded funds. These are indexes full of list of companies in specific industries and can found by conducting an online search like 'industry tech ETF'. Make your way down the list of companies, see which companies are doing well and which ones you're interested in, and then list them up.

Now, get to work learning everything you can about these companies. Bookmark relevant pages for news of their websites, follow them on social media and highlight news links that contain news and updates from them. You may even want to set up Google Alert notifications, so you know exactly when something is posted on them.

You can also use a screener app or profile that can filter stocks in the world based on criteria you enter, such as the industry they're in, their value, or a specific sector. Finally, you can simply look at the graphs and stock exchanges and find companies that appeal to you. Since you'll already have some kind of interest in the industry, you've probably got an idea of some companies you'd like to be working with.

Using Qualitative Data

Qualitative data is a term you'll see thrown around the stock market and among traders which basically refers to the type of news and media we've covered above, plus a little extra. This is all the external information you're looking at, such as company news that you see online, on TV, or through the company itself, as well as detailed events.

These detailed events can include things like changes in a company's personnel line up, and financial events surrounding the company. For example, suppose a company is planning to restructure, and you see the news that a company is potentially hiring one of the leading marketing executives in the world. In that case, this could be a sign the company could make a lot of money in the near future, meaning now could be an excellent time to buy. Likewise, if a manager or executive steps down unexpectedly, this could cause the stock to fall, so you'll need to get in the know as quickly as possible so you can react with strategy.

In terms of financial events, look for things like the COVID-19 pandemic or large-scale events like Brexit. All these events impact the stock market one way or another, so it's essential to make sure you take these factors into considerations.

Using Quantitative Data

Quantitative data is a significant section of data to look at because this will highlight the inner workings of a company, giving you everything you need to see whether it's a healthy stock you want to invest in.

Under this umbrella term, you'll find data streams like the earning's sheets from a company, the balance sheets, the ratios, and the dividends. Here's a table that explains it all very nicely.

Earning Sheets	Refers to the earnings that a company has, whether that's losses or profits. If a company is experiencing drops on their earnings sheet, this could show the company is unhealthy and you won't want to buy stock. Likewise, sometimes a stock may not reflect this drop of earnings straight away, which means you'll want to be careful when trading it.

Balance Sheets	This is a document that will contain all the liabilities and assets a company has. The healthier and stronger this sheet is, the more reliable and stable the stock tends to be, especially when you consider these assets should translate into potential earnings.
Ratios	There are plenty of ratios out there which mean different things, refer to different aspects of a company, and provide different metrics. To find out more, refer to the table below.
Dividends	This figure refers to the segment of a company's profit that will be returned to its shareholders. If a company is finding hard to pay back their shareholders, this could be a clear sign the company is suffering, and you'll want to exercise caution when purchasing this stock.

There's a ton of ratios you can consider when it comes to choosing or avoiding a stock, so here's a quick lowdown to keep you in the know.

Price-to-Earnings Ratio (P/E)	A simple metric that details how much money you would need to spend to make $1 of profit on this stock. This is a fantastic metric to use when comparing the stocks between different companies in the same sector.
Debt-Equity Ratio (D/E)	This ratio adds up all the assets a company has and compares it with how much debt the company has.
Return on Equity (ROE)	This is a percentage ratio that shows how much profit a company can make with the equity it has. It will show whether a company can standalone with its profits or relies on shareholder's contributions and investments.
Price-Earnings to Growth (PEG)	This ratio takes the Price-to-Earnings ratio above and compares it with growth in the annual EPS, showing it as a percentage. This is a great way to tell if a stock has a fair value or not.

Price-to-Book (P/B) Ratio	Another simple metric ratio that shows whether the market price of stock matches up with the company's book value for its stock. If the ratio is high, this means the company is overvaluing themselves.
Current Ratio	This ratio looks at a company's ability to pay off their debts. It takes into consideration their assets and liabilities. If the ratio is low, then the chances are the stock value is going to go down as well.

You don't need to know all these metrics, nor use them all when deciding whether a stock is a right choice or not, but if you're aware that all these metrics exist. They are incredibly helpful when it comes to choosing which stocks you want to buy and making sure you can trust the prices you're seeing on the stock exchange itself. With all this in mind, you can use the metrics you want to be as informed as possible when implementing your day trading strategy.

Chapter 10 - Beginner Day Trading Stock Market Strategies You Need to Know

While it's all well and good being able to pick and choose stocks that will make you money, the trick to becoming an actual successful day trader comes down to your ability to do two things; maximise your profits and minimise your losses.

We've said this before, but we'll repeat it for clarity, there are very few traders of any kind that will make millions overnight, not without a ridiculously big investment. Real success as a trader comes the ability to make steady and consistent wins over a long period of time, minimising the cost of your losses as much as possible to retain your profit.

This means you need a strategy.

In this chapter, we're going to explore some of the key strategies you need to know about as a beginner day trader, helping you see what sort of work you should be doing, and therefore what kind of direction you'll be heading in.

Get Educated. Knowledge is Everything.

You've probably heard of the saying' knowledge is power', and it's true, especially when it comes to trading on the stock market of any kind. The more you know about a stock, the company, the conditions of the economy, and the industry you're buying in, the more educated a choice you'll be able to make.

This means getting educated. This means you need to be reading magazines and articles, watching news reports, and following a company's social media profiles and seeing what's going on.

For example, if you had money in Tesla stock back in September 2018, you would have paid attention to the face that Joe Rogan was interviewing the CEO Elon Musk on his famous YouTube podcast. Knowing this, you should have been watching the live stream podcast, and you would see that Elon smoked marijuana on the show, causing the stock to drop by 30% off its intraday high.

As a day trader, its events like this that are happening in real-time that you need to be thinking about and paying attention too. Let's say you already have stock in Tesla. When something like this happens, you have three choices. Are you;

A. Going to sell your Tesla stock ASAP because the stock value is dropping.

B. Buy more Tesla stocks because you believe the market is going to bounce back, and you can make money from this dip in the stock's value.

C. Do nothing.

There's no right or wrong answer to this. If you have Tesla stocks, then we'll assume you'll have an understanding of the tech and electric car industry, so you'll need to make an educated decision. Electric cars are gaining popularity. Head over to Twitter and see what the social impact of the event had on the reputation of Tesla. What is Tesla planning to do about it?

Of course, this happened two years ago, and the intraday high at the time was $381. As of August 2020, the intraday high since is now sitting around the $2,049 mark, meaning if you had bought all the stocks when they lost their 30% value, you would have made a lot of money.

This is why you need to be educated in your industry and niches, the companies you're investing in, and being able to see patterns between real-time events and stock values.

Trade at the Right Times

When the stock market opens at the beginning of the day, a lot of day traders and investors will already know precisely what they want to do and will place their orders and trades literally the minute trade commences. However, this can contribute drastically to price volatility, and as a beginner day trader, you might not know how to deal with these fluctuations.

Instead, a great strategy to implement is not to make any trades within 15 to 20 minutes of the market opening. In fact, it can even pay to wait until around midday to start your trades since the markets are less volatile and activity is then starting to pick up again towards the end of the trading day.

Sure, there are opportunities to made during this time, but when you're just starting out, and you're learning the basics and managing the ropes, it's best off avoided. Instead, use this free time to watch the markets, get educated on what's going on, and then make your purchasing decisions later in the day.

Minimise Your Losses with Limit Orders

There are two main types of order you can get involved with when entering and exiting trades. Market orders, where you buy a stock, make the payment, and the stock is yours – the generic form of order – and then there's limit orders. Limit orders are a great way to minimise your losses, especially when you're starting out.

When you buy using a market order, you're merely buying a stock at the price which is best available at the time, which could be anything, also meaning there's no guarantee. On the other hand, a limit order means you can guarantee the price, but you don't have to go through with the order itself.

With a limit order, you can select the price you want to buy at, making sure you're actually picking a realistic price, and the price you want to sell out. This is a great way to minimise your losses because you're trading with precision. You know exactly what price you're buying at, and then what price you're selling at.

Of course, there's no way to guarantee that these prices are ever going to get met. You can't say you're going to buy a $1,000 stock when it gets to $400, because the chances are that's never going to happen. When using limit orders, you may need to develop your experience over what you set your limits as, but this will come in time.

Remember Your Profit Percentage

It's vital to remember that you can't trade and win every single trade. Even the most experienced of traders who have been in the business for decades will only win between 50% and 60% of their investments, and that's on a good day. This means you don't want to be aiming for a 100%-win rate because you're only going to find yourself disheartened.

I'm going to keep saying this because it's just so important, and it's trading 1-0-1 that you operate to this strategy rule. You need to aim to maximise your profits and minimise your losses, not just aim to win big all the time and never lose. That's not how this works.

Follow the Bull Flag Strategy

The bull flag strategy is an excellent strategy for beginners and a great one for making money. First, you need to find a stock that is soaring on a high volume, relative to the stock you're looking at. Look at this stock long-term, perhaps over the last five years and make sure the over trend is upwards. These are the ideal stocks for this strategy.

So, you've found a bull flag stock. Now zoom into its five-minute chart and see whether the stock is still experiencing an upward trend. All you need to do now is wait for the stock to consolidate, and you need to make sure this consolidation is at a lower volume than the upward movement.

As you can see, this is rather simple. You're buying a stock and entering the trade when the stock breaks above the consolidation pattern (when it has a higher volume) and you're exiting the trade when your stock is below the bottom of the consolidation pattern we mentioned above.

Again, if you're starting out, you may want to practice this with some smaller funds just to get the hang of identifying the stocks and their breakout zones, but don't worry if it all sounds confusing to begin with. Once you've practised a few times and you know what you're looking for, you'll have this strategy down in no time.

The Momentum Trading Strategy

The Momentum Trading Strategy is perhaps the most popular form of day trading and the core of what you're going to be doing in your day-to-day trading operations. The stock market works in a way there are a ton of stocks that will increase their value by 20% to 30% per day. Yes, it sounds incredible, but when you consider the gains and losses over time, then the growth of a stock is relatively balanced.

However, there are peaks and valleys in the growth process, and the job of a momentum trader is to ride the growth of the stock all the way to the top as close to that summit as you can before selling everything and investing that money and investment into a new stock that is currently on its way up.

That, in its very purest form, is how momentum trading works.

It's all about finding stocks that are on their way up, finding new stocks that also look like they're going to rise, and then when the first stock is just about to peak, you sell and invest in your second stock.

Some stocks will be easier to do this with than others. If you look at some stocks, they may start growing as the market opens and peak around midday before heading back down again to the end of the day. If this happens every single day for a month, then you can see this as a pattern you can profit from, although bear in mind that others will have already noticed this trend which can then make it unpredictable.

As with all these strategies, it takes practice to be able to see what's going on and having the ability to notice patterns and potential opportunities but being able to do this will all come with experience.

These are just some of the many strategies you can get involved with as a day trader, and the chances are you're going to be using a mixture of them all, depending on what real-time opportunities you're being presented with. Try them out for yourself, start small, expand your experience and then aim to grow and get bigger and bigger over time.

Chapter 11 - How to Manage Your Investments and Portfolio

As we come towards the end of our journey and you're ready to push the boat out and take control of your own day trader journey, these final chapters will be looking at tips and tricks you need to know as a day trader, as well as covering what you need to be thinking about as you head into the future.

To start with, we're going to be exploring how to manage your investments and your portfolio. Your portfolio is, of course, the stocks that you're buying and selling. Imagine a folder containing 10-15 stocks that you've purchased. This is your portfolio, but how do you manage it safely and securely? This is what we're going to explore here.

Create a Safety Margin

One of the first things you should do is create a safety margin which can help you to protect your investments. This is by far one of the most important and most essential ways to secure yourself. Fortunately, there are two ways you can do this.

Firstly, you can ensure you're making conservative valuations in the assumptions you're making. Of course, the main process of a day trader is to make assumptions on a stock's value, based on the information and patterns you're seeing. By being conservative in these valuations, you're ensuring you're creating a safety blanket by not going too far with your estimates and ultimately entering a danger zone.

This can happen at both ends of the scale. When your trades are right, and you're making money, you can easily fall into the trap of being incredibly optimistic with your valuations that make you want to invest more with the aim of making more. However, when things are on the up for a mediocre business, you're putting your investment in danger.

Put it this way, there's little risk you can overpay for an excellent business, but a very high risk you'll overpay for a mediocre one. Let's look into an example of this.

Let's say you're investing in a business that has stocks valued at $100 per share in profit which are then worth $108 with 8% growth. However, if you're predicting the growth rate is going to be 15%, valuing the stock at $115, this means you've overpaid the stock because you'll only be making half the profit you intended.

Instead, being able to be more conservative with your assumptions mean you won't be making that mistake. If you predict the growth of our example to be 10%, 8% isn't so bad, and if you do hit 15% growth, then that's a bonus.

The second approach you can take is making sure you choose which stocks you are buying carefully. It's so easy to see a hive of activity taking place around one stock, and in the excitement of it all, it's something you want to get involved in, so you jump on board. However, just because a lot of people are doing it, that doesn't make it right.

You also need to consider the intrinsic value of your stocks and making sure they are stocks that suit your budget. If you're trading with $10,000 and you buy ten stocks at $1,000 each, then this isn't a very safe investment. If the stock drops, you've lost everything.

This is why it pays to have diversity in your portfolio, which is all included when you're thinking about choosing your stocks carefully. Think about the values of stocks and what sort of money you're going to be making, once again creating that margin for safety.

For example, if you have a stock which is valued at $10, you don't want to be buying it when it's valued at $9 because that's only a stock with a 10% safety margin. Instead, buying it at $6 gives you a 40% safety margin.

Always Measuring Operating Performance

The majority of investors find themselves caught in a candid trap. They end up looking at the current market price of a stock and take that metric as all they need to know when it comes to validating and measuring their purchases and trades, but in doing so, they miss a fundamental metric. This is the underlying performance of the asset.

While this is something that will tend to affect more long-term investments, it's still worth checking the operating performance of a stock before making a purchase. If a stock is extremely volatile, and this is clear from the operating performance, and you don't check it, you could end up losing a lot of money over a short amount of time. It's always better to be safe than sorry.

Only Invest in What You Know

As we said above, it can be tempting to get drawn into investments with mouth-watering returns because everyone is going on about them and because they look good. If you don't know the market and you don't understand the companies, then you're basically throwing your investment into uncharted waters, and the risks here are huge.

Reading this now, you're probably thinking that this is just common sense, but when you're in the moment, and everything is happening so fast, it's easy to get caught up in the whirlwind of it and make the mistake of investing when you probably shouldn't.

Yes, you may be looking at an opportunity and thinking 'yes, this is a fantastic opportunity and I want to make some money on it. I can't miss it.' You need to have enough discipline to be able to say no and that the trade is too risky because you don't know enough about it. By making decisions like this, you're coming off your strategy, and even it pays off once, you've ruined your boundary that will stop you doing it again, and that's where things get dangerous.

This is what it means to be a successful stock trader. You need to make sure you're well aware of your strengths and your weaknesses and then be able to take steps accordingly to maximise your profits and minimise your losses.

· These are just some of the best ways to manage and protect your investments and your portfolio. You'd be surprised with how much this final tip is missed, but if you don't use your common sense and you let emotions get in the way of your practices, you're going to have a bad time, and you'll soon find yourself facing problems.

Chapter 12 - Essential Day Trading and Money Management Tips

The final chapter of this book could be seen as one of the most important. We've looked into how to trade and what kind of mindset you need, as well as how to protect your investments and trade safely, but this final point is looking how to manage your money in the best possible way.

This is somewhat similar to the previous chapter, but. In contrast, those are general trading tips that every trader will be putting into practice or at least should be, this chapter we're going to be looking at day trader specifics, especially when it comes to money management.

At the end of the day, even a trader who's trading with a 70% win rate can lose everything when not managing their money correctly on the remaining 30%. Likewise, even a trader with a 40% win rate could be making a ton of money, even when losing 60% of their trades, due to their excellent money management skills.

Let's begin.

Create a Stop-Loss Max Dollar Mark

As part of your strategy, you'll want to set up a stop-loss mark that is basically your stopping point for trading each and every day. There are always going to tempting offers that draw you in for the wrong reasons, and even if you've been trading all day, you need to be at a point where you know when to stop.

As a rule of thumb, you'll want to stop your max-dollar stop-loss point somewhere between two to three times your average daily profits, and that's if you're working with a high win-ratio. Again, make sure you're using your common sense to set this mark to one that works for you. If your win rate starts to drop, then you'll want to think about dropping this stop-loss mark as well to remain safe.

Yes, it takes discipline to put this practice into, well, practice, but it's essential you do so. Otherwise, you could end up blowing all your account on some dodgy trades, and you'll be out of business for good.

Always Take Breaks

It's all well and good when you find your flow and get stuck into the mindset of making profits and really feeling as though you're one with the stock exchange, but without taking breaks, you're only going to end up screwing yourself.

Being a day trader in such a fast-paced world is no easy feat, and it's going to take its toll on your psychology. Having dedicated and necessary breaks are an essential part of being able to keep your emotions out of the game, and your head and mind focused on the task at hand. Even if you're taking ten minutes to get outside, get some water, walk around the block, and take a breath, this is far better than just sitting and staring at your computer screen all day.

Depending on how much you're working, you'll want to take a ten-minute break minimum, but they could be anywhere up to several hours. In stressful situations, let's say you've just been on a huge winning streak or a massive losing spiral, these can be the most emotional of times, so turning off your computer and being away from the game for a day or two just to let your head get back to a neutral headspace could be one of the best decisions you make.

Find Stocks with a Solid Risk/Reward Ratio

Don't worry, this is the last time I'm going to say this, but day trading is all about maximising your profits and minimising your losses. Such a rare group of investors will make a ton of money off one single trade and get-rich-quick thinking like this will only be your downfall. Again, last time we're going to say that, so hoping it's gone in.

With this in mind, you're going to want to be looking at a handful of stocks that have a stable risk/reward ratio, basically saying that you know you're going to win the trade. Of course, you can never guarantee this is going to happen, and there will always be exceptions to the rule, but there are golden stocks out there that reliably win and grow, even if it's by a small and steady amount.

Typically, this works by you looking for a stock where the risk/reward ratio is where the potential profit of your trade is higher than the loss. Ideally, you'll want this to sit around the 2:1 mark, 3:1 if you can find a stock like this.

You then need to think about what is the probability that you're going to hit this ratio before the stop-loss is hit. If you're working out that the likelihood that a trade is going to be successful is around 80%, then go for it, but if the probability is smaller, then you need to be careful about how much you're investing.

You can minimise your losses by reducing how much capital you're investing, and then making sure your timings are right, i.e. getting in quickly, and then getting out again just as quick. Little wins go a long way in the day trading world.

Always Average Up and Never Average Down

We spoke about this briefly in the last chapter, but it's well worth covering again just so it's clear. Don't be considerate with your averages. When you're working out the potential average loss you could be working with, never make it too low. Always average up, just to be on the safe side.

If you ever find yourself at a weak point and you're averaging down on your predicted losses, this is a great way to blow your load and end your account. Yes, many traders will do this because they're trying to reassure and validate themselves that everything is going to be okay.

If you're saying things like 'oh yes, this is only going to be a 10% loss maximum, so everything is going to be fine', but it turns out the loss was 20%, this is double what you predicted and could be catastrophic for your account. Instead, if you had averaged up and played around the prediction it was going to be 15%, then the hit won't have been too hard.

Avoid Trades of Higher Risk

While there definitely profits to be made with high-risk trades, they are obviously called high-risk trades for a reason. The losses can be devastating, and when you think that most of the time you're going to find yourself making high-risk plays because you've just faced huge losses and you're trying to make your money back, these trades look even worse.

Of course, if you're in a comfortable position and you really feel good about a high-risk trade because you've educated yourself and you believe you know what you're doing, then go for gold on it, and you're wished all the best. Sometimes, these plays do come off. However, always consider your position before getting involved to ensure you're taking this risk for the right reasons, not out of desperation.

Be Cautious After a Losing Streak

Hand in hand with the consideration above, it's essential to think about what kind of mindset you're in after you've faced a stream of substantial losses. This can be an incredibly emotional and stressful time, and if you've lost a considerable percentage of your investment, it's only human nature that you're going to want to win it all back.

While it can be tempting to go beyond your stop-loss mark, make high-risk trades, and make plays you would never typically make, you need to stop, take a breather, and not do what you're about to do. We're hoping that reading this will set the seed you need to bring awareness to your mind when this happens because you're almost guaranteed to find yourself in this position.

When you're facing a losing streak, the best thing you can do is pack up and set away from the computer. Take a breather and get your mind back to a focused and clear point of very. Even the biggest, most successful traders in the world will go through periods of substantial loss, and these times is what separates the successful traders from the mediocre ones.

Keep Your Ego Out of the Equation

Do you agree with this statement? Is it better never to have money at all than to have profited and then lost everything? Why is this true? Because of your ego. It's human nature and instinct to want to be a winner. To want to look at over traders and think yes, I'm a winner compared to these people.

Nobody wants to be a loser, and just like the consideration above, this kind of thinking can lead you to make stupid decisions. Keep your ego out of your trading practices. Whether you're just being aware of your thinking or you're practising mindfulness meditation, it doesn't matter.

What matters is that you notice how your mind is working, what thoughts are going through your head, and then understanding whether these thought patterns are serving you or holding you back from doing what's right. Yes, this all sounds very spirituality, but when you think about it, the primitive human brain isn't designed to make good decisions on something like the stock market, it wants to do what humans do best, which is to survive and be the best in their competitive environment.

Rid yourself of these attachments and focus on what's important, make the right decisions, and be the best day trader you can be.

Chapter 13 - Heading into the Future & Final Words

That brings us to the final chapter of our book, and the end of your introduction into the world of day trading. Hopefully you've had a solid journey so far, and you're ready to go it alone and turn your dream of trading on the stock market into a full-time career.

As you head off into the future of your new life, remember, keep your head on your shoulders and stay as grounded as possible. There's nothing worse or riskier than a stressful and emotional trader who's making all the wrong decisions because they've lost control. Stay in control.

Also, remember that you can never stop learning. There are always going to be ways to enhance your skills and better your experience. Most of your success will come from starting small and building on your experience of the stock market.

Make sure you're taking time to follow the leaders of the day trading world and seeing what they do, but most importantly asking why they do what they do, and then learning how to incorporate their tactics into your own practices.

Stay headstrong and keep your eyes on the prize. Good luck, work hard and believe in yourself. Let this be the first steps you take on a long and bright road into your profitable and productive future.

Printed in Great Britain
by Amazon